An Educational Coloring Book of CATS

EDITOR
Linda Spizzirri

ILLUSTRATIONS
Peter M. Spizzirri

COVER ART
Peter M. Spizzirri

CONTENTS

HISTORY OF THE CAT	Page 2
DIAGRAM OF THE CAT	Page 3
AMERICAN SHORT-HAIR *(Felis catus)*	Page 4
ABYSSINIAN *(Felis catus)*	Page 6
RUSSIAN BLUE *(Felis catus)*	Page 8
ANGORA *(Felis catus)*	Page 10
BURMESE *(Felis catus)*	Page 12
MANX *(Felis catus)*	Page 14
PERSIAN *(Felis catus)*	Page 16
CORNISH REX *(Felis catus)*	Page 18
SIAMESE *(Felis catus)*	Page 20
BRITISH SHORT-HAIR TABBY *(Felis catus)*	Page 22
SPHYNX *(Felis catus)*	Page 24
MAINE COON CAT *(Felis catus)*	Page 26
JAPANESE BOBTAIL *(Felis catus)*	Page 28
TURKISH CAT *(Felis catus)*	Page 30

Copyright, ©, 1985 by Spizzirri Publishing, Inc., All rights reserved.

An Educational Coloring Book of CATS • Published by SPIZZIRRI PUBLISHING, INC., P.O. BOX 9397, RAPID CITY, SOUTH DAKOTA 57709. No part of this publication may be reproduced by any means without the express written consent of the publisher. All national and international rights reserved on the entire contents of this publication.
Printed in U.S.A.

HISTORY OF THE CAT

Small creatures that were the ancestors of the cat, inhabited the prehistoric forests about 55 million years ago. These small creatures spred to inhabit the entire world. The desert cat species, *Dinictis*, developed and increased in numbers. It is this desert cat that is the common ancestor of all domestic cats. As far back as 8 million years ago, it had developed to resemble the domestic cat of today.

The cat was domesticated around 1800 B.C., probably because of the cat's ability to eliminate rodents. Keeping rats and mice away from the grains needed for food was a very important task.

The cat was most popular in Egypt. It not only controlled rodents in the graineries and in the house, but was also considered a house pet. If a cat should die, the owners would mourn the loss and even shave their eyebrows to show their sorrow. Some cats were mummified, as humans were in Egypt, and found centuries later when the Pyramids were opened. The Egyptian nobility and priests cherished their cats as pets and as insights into the gods. Cats were even worshipped as the gods Bast and Sekhmet. The Egyptians also took great care in breeding their cats so that the little kittens would be desirable.

It is believed the domestic Egyptian cat was brought to Asia by the Hykos. They obtained the cats while at war in Egypt. Breeding these cats with other species probably gave rise to the long-hair cats we have today. The interest in cats and their selective breeding also spred to the Orient.

Phoenician trading vessels brought cats to Europe about 900 B.C. They were immediately popular as a means of rodent control, both in the graineries and especially in the house during the time of the Black Plague.

European explorers, who kept cats aboard ship, brought the cat to America. It immediately became popular both to the American settlers and American Indians. They used it to control rodents around their homes and in their stores of maize (corn). The popularity of cats as household pets has been increasing for centuries. They are probably more popular today than ever before.

CAT SHOWS AND COMPETITIONS

There are a great many cat clubs and organizations which hold competitions to judge outstanding individuals in each breed. Most cat shows judge in the following classes:

1. Kittens - for kittens 4-8 months old.
2. Novice - for cats who have not received a first prize in competition.
3. Open - for cats who have not won a championship in competition.
4. Championship - for those cats who have won four or more ribbons in competition.
5. Grand Champion - for cats who have won championships and are earning points toward Grand Champion.

The largest of the cat shows is in London, England. Every year about 2,000 cats are entered in both pedigree and pet categories. Cat shows are also popular in the United States. With the increased interested in cats as pets and for show, cats have been bred with greater and greater care, producing very beautiful animals.

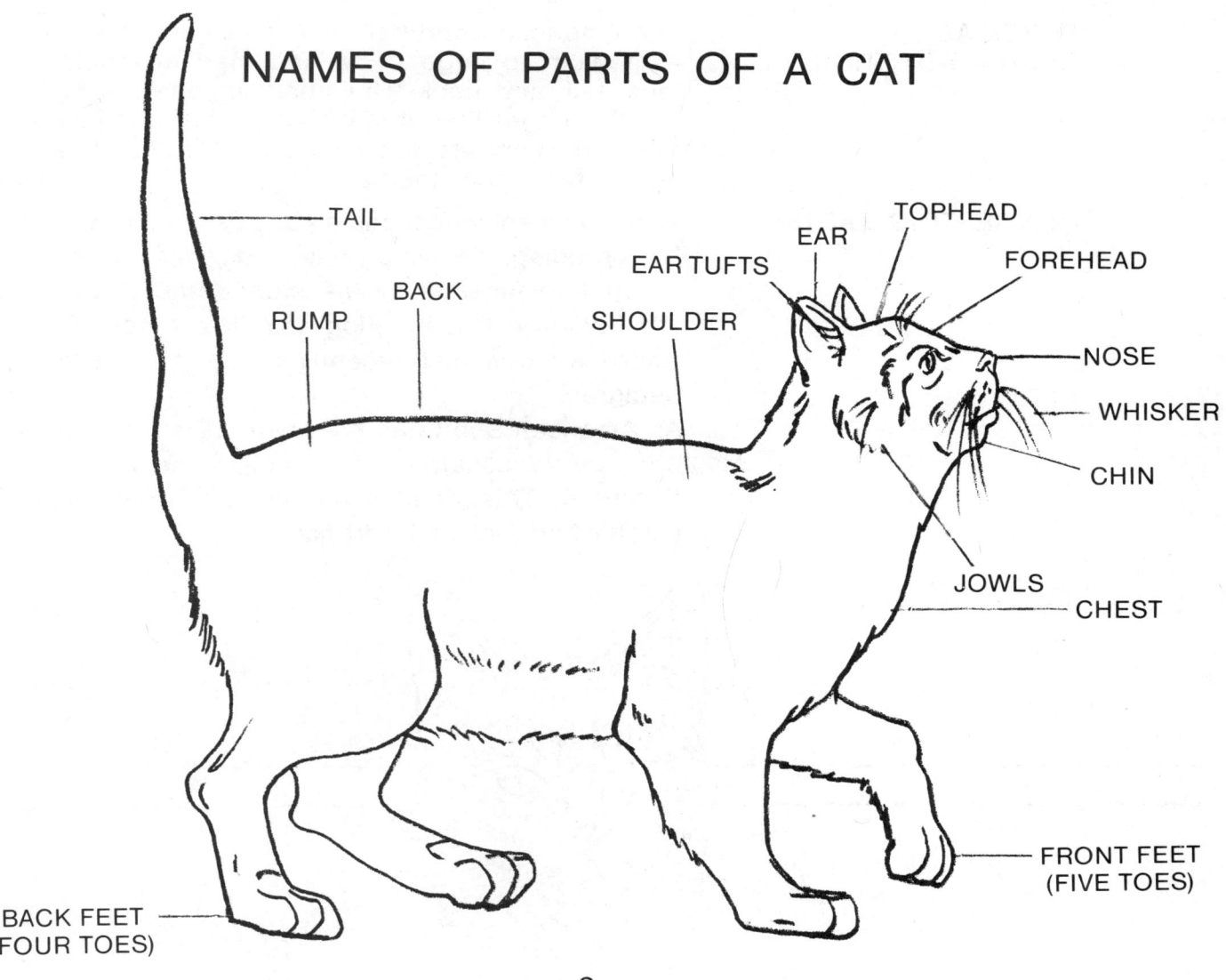

NAMES OF PARTS OF A CAT

NAME:	AMERICAN SHORT-HAIR, DOMESTIC SHORT-HAIR *(Felis catus)*
WHERE THE BREED DEVELOPED:	UNITED STATES
COLOR IT:	SOLID BLUE, BLACK, WHITE, RED-BROWN, AND CREME. THESE COLORS CAN BE SHADED BY SILVER-GRAY, DARK GRAY, LIGHT BLUE-TAN, AND CALICO (tortoiseshell and white). ALSO CAN BE PATCHES OR STRIPES OF THE SAME COLORS.
PHYSICAL CHARACTERISTICS:	The American Short-hair is a well-built cat with a medium to large body, and medium-length legs, tail, and neck. The head appears to be slightly longer than it is wide (oblong). Both its eyes and ears are set wide apart. The coat is short, thick, and coarse.
INTERESTING FACTS:	This intelligent, affectionate cat was established by breeding the short-hair cats, that were brought to America by the early settlers, with the pedigree British Short-hair. The American Short-hair was just recently recognized as a pedigree. An American Short-hair bred with a Persian cat produces a separate breed called the Exotic Short-hair. This breed is very close to the long-established British Short-hair.

NAME:	ABYSSINIAN *(Felis catus)*
WHERE THE BREED DEVELOPED:	ABYSSINIA (NOW ETHIOPIA, AFRICA)
COLOR IT:	SOLID ORANGE-BROWN WITH NO BARS OR WHITE MARKINGS. NOSE IS BRICK-RED, OUTLINED IN BLACK. LIGHT (CREME) COLOR AROUND MOUTH AND EYES.
PHYSICAL CHARACTERISTICS:	This short-haired cat has a long, slender body and a long, tapering tail. It has slender legs and oval feet. The wedge-shaped head has ears that are large at the base and pointed at the tip.
INTERESTING FACTS:	This sleek cat is affectionate and highly intelligent, but independent. It needs room to roam, and will become unhappy if confined. The Abyssinian was brought to America in the early 1900's from Britain, but did not enjoy immediate popularity. Today, however, there are more Abyssinians in America than in Britain and they are in great demand. They are hard to obtain because the female gives birth to a small litter of four kittens or less. The Abyssinian looks like the cats shown in Egyptian art, but there is no evidence to support the claim that it is a direct descendant of the cats of the Pharaohs.

NAME:	RUSSIAN BLUE *(Felis catus)*
WHERE THE BREED DEVELOPED:	RUSSIA
COLOR IT:	A CLEAR BLUE-GRAY COLOR WITH A SILVER-GRAY CAST. BRIGHT GREEN EYES.
PHYSICAL CHARACTERISTICS:	These short-haired cats have long, graceful bodies with a long, tapering tail, long legs, and small, oval feet. Its almond-shaped eyes are set far apart in a wedge-shaped head. The ears are wide at the base and rounded at the tip. One of its distinguishing features is the very thin skin on the ears, which is almost thin enough to see through.
INTERESTING FACTS:	This beautiful cat was commonly called the Archangel cat after the Russian port where British sailors first obtained it. This gentle cat becomes very attached to its owner and doesn't seem to mind not having a lot of room in which to roam. The Russian Blue was introduced to the United States in the early 1900's but did not achieve any recognition until after World War II.

NAME:	ANGORA *(Felis catus)*
WHERE THE BREED DEVELOPED:	ANGORA (NOW ANKARA), TURKEY
COLOR IT:	WHITE COAT. EYES ARE BLUE, AMBER, OR ODD-EYE (one eye of each color). PINK NOSE.
PHYSICAL CHARACTERISTICS:	This cat has a small to medium size body and head. The head is wide between the ears and tapers to a point at the chin. Its medium-long coat is of silky-soft, fine hair. The full tail is long and tapering. The hind legs are slightly longer than the front legs.
INTERESTING FACTS:	This cat, a goat, and a rabbit all bear the name Angora after this city in Turkey where they are thought to originate. As a matter of fact, all long-hair cats were called "Angora" at one time. This pure white cat was almost extinct, and is not recognized in Britain as a breed. A pair of Angoras were sent from Turkey in 1963 and 1966 to re-introduce the breed to America and, by 1970, it was accepted. It is a lovely white cat that can have blue eyes but, like all white cats, if they have blue eyes, they are likely to be deaf.

NAME:	BURMESE (*Felis catus*)
WHERE THE BREED DEVELOPED:	GENERALLY ACCEPTED TO BE OF ASIAN ORIGIN
COLOR IT:	ORIGINAL HYBRID WAS BROWN. MODIFICATION OF THE GENES HAVE PRODUCED BLUE, LIGHT CHOCOLATE-BROWN, RED-BROWN, LILAC-GRAY, TAN (CREME), AND TORTOISESHELL BREEDS. EYES ARE DEEP GOLDEN YELLOW.
PHYSICAL CHARACTERISTICS:	The head of the Burmese is rounded on top, between ears that are set far apart, and tilted slightly forward. The muscular body is of medium length and size, with a medium-length tail that tapers to a slightly rounded tip. The back is straight from shoulder to rump even though the hind legs are longer than the front legs. The large eyes are set far apart. The coat has fine, satin-like short hair.
INTERESTING FACTS:	These beautiful cats were said to have been the pride of the aristocracy and priests of Burma. Legend has it that each cat had its own human servant! Actually, it cannot be proven that this cat came from Burma. Its ancestors were an unidentified, dark-colored breed and a Siamese cat. This breed was imported to the United States from India in 1936. They are intelligent and friendly cats, that are not as high-strung as their Siamese ancestors.

NAME:	MANX *(Felis catus)*
WHERE THE BREED DEVELOPED:	ISLE OF MAN IN THE IRISH SEA
COLOR IT:	ANY SOLID COLOR OR PATTERNED BI-COLOR. EYE COLOR SHOULD COMPLEMENT COAT COLOR.
PHYSICAL CHARACTERISTICS:	This cat is similar to any standard short-hair cat, but it does have two features that make it very easy to recognize. It has no tail and it has a coat that is soft and open with a thick undercoat, like a rabbit's fur. The back is short and the long hind legs make the rump set very high. The ears are set well apart on a rounded head.
INTERESTING FACTS:	Legends describe some very interesting ways that this cat lost its tail. One explanation is that Noah got impatient and slammed the door of the ark shut, cutting the poor cat's tail off. It is unfortunate that the same mutation that makes the cat tailless also makes it susceptible to vertebrae, muscle, and nerve problems. The long, powerful hind legs of the Manx make it walk with a distinctive "bob," and also make it the best jumper of the domestic cats.

NAME:	PERSIAN OR LONG-HAIR *(Felis catus)*
WHERE THE BREED DEVELOPED:	PERSIA OR ANGORA (IS NOT DEFINITELY PROVEN)
COLOR IT:	PERSIANS CAN BE BLACK, WHITE, RED-BROWN, TAN (CREME), BLUISH-CREME, SILVER, GRAY (SMOKE) OR MULTI-COLORED COMBINATIONS. ONLY THE WHITE PERSIAN HAS BLUE EYES, ALL OTHER BREEDS HAVE DEEP ORANGE OR COPPER EYES.
PHYSICAL CHARACTERISTICS:	The numerous Persian breeds all have long hair that is thick and silky. The body is large, solid, and cobby (meaning it has short legs and is broad). The head is round with full cheeks and large, round eyes. It has well-tufted tail and ears.
INTERESTING FACTS:	People are very attracted to this intelligent, affectionate pet with its beautiful long, full coat. The original Persian cat was a result of breeding an Egyptian Short-hair with a wild long-hair variety. The resulting long-hair had the "tabby" markings that are found in the wild cat types. Centuries of controlled breeding produced Persians that have solid color coats, and the eye color has changed. The result is that we now have a large color variety in the Persian breed. In the cat family, if breeding for color is not carefully controlled, the coat color will soon revert to its original "tabby" coloring.

NAME:	CORNISH REX *(Felix catus)*
WHERE THE BREED DEVELOPED:	CORNWALL, ENGLAND
COLOR IT:	ANY COAT COLOR IS ACCEPTABLE.
PHYSICAL CHARACTERISTICS:	The Cornish Rex has a slender, muscular body and long, straight legs. The ears are very large and set high on its wedge-shaped head. The very distinctive coat is curly. The tail is long, thin, and also covered with curly hair.
INTERESTING FACTS:	The first Cornish Rex was born in England in 1950. No pure American strain was ever developed.
	No other cat has this unusual coat. Most cats have different kinds of hairs making up their coats, while the Cornish Rex has only down hairs that curl. Some people refer to this cat as the "Poodle Cat," because the hair curls like a Poodle's. People who have this breed like the fact that loose hairs are held in the coat. This makes it a very clean pet.

NAME:	SIAMESE *(Felis catus)*
WHERE THE BREED DEVELOPED:	THAILAND (SIAM), ALTHOUGH CANNOT BE ABSOLUTELY PROVEN
COLOR IT:	THE SEAL POINT WAS THE FIRST, AND ONLY, SIAMESE TO BE RECOGNIZED FOR A LONG TIME. ITS COAT IS TAN (CREME) WITH DARK BROWN (SEAL) COLORED POINTS (EARS, FACE, PAWS, AND TAIL). OTHER BREEDS HAVE BEEN ACCEPTED WITH CREME OR WHITE COATS AND OTHER THAN DARK BROWN (SEAL) POINTS. EYES ARE CLEAR, DEEP BLUE.
PHYSICAL CHARACTERISTICS:	This elegant cat has short, fine, sleek hair that lays close to a slender body. The long, tapering tail is thin, even at the base. The long head has oriental-shaped, slanting eyes that are set far apart. The large ears are wide at the base and pointed at the tips.
INTERESTING FACTS:	These legendary temple cats of Thailand were brought to Britain and the United States in the late 1800's. They now rank as the most popular cat in the United States. The reasons they are so popular are: they are intelligent; active; affectionate; and, in general, are very alert and inquisitive about what goes on around them. They also become very attached to their owners.

NAME:	BRITISH SHORT-HAIR TABBY (*Felis catus*)
WHERE THE BREED DEVELOPED:	BRITAIN
COLOR IT:	BROWN WITH BLACK MARKINGS, SILVER-GRAY WITH BLACK MARKINGS, ORANGE-BROWN WITH DARKER REDDISH-BROWN MARKINGS.
PHYSICAL CHARACTERISTICS:	The British Short-hair Tabby is a strong-boned, medium-size cat whose coat is short and fine. Its thick body is set on short, well-proportioned legs. The tail is thick and tapers only slightly at the tip. The "apple-shaped" head has small ears and larger, round eyes.
INTERESTING FACTS:	This familiar striped or patterned cat is called "Tabby" after a watered-silk cloth that has the same patterned effect. This silk is known as "tabby cloth." The pattern on the Tabby's face forms a characteristic "M" on the forehead, which legend says is a tribute to the prophet Mohammed. The British Tabby was brought to America by the early settlers. The American descendants of the British Tabby have the familiar "tabby" patterned coat, but have developed into their own separate and distinctly different breed.

NAME:	SPHYNX OR CANADIAN HAIRLESS (*Felis catus*)
WHERE THE BREED DEVELOPED:	ONTARIO, CANADA
COLOR IT:	ANY SOLID OR MULTI-COLOR. GOLDEN EYES.
PHYSICAL CHARACTERISTICS:	The Sphynx has a hairless body that is long and muscular. The large ears are far apart on the outward-sloping head. The skin is smooth and only wrinkles around the head. It has short, "velvety" hairs on the points: around the face and back of the ears; wrist; ankle; and the last inch of the long, thin tail.
INTERESTING FACTS:	It was not until 1960 that the first Sphynx hairless was born to a black and white house cat in Ontario, Canada. It is from this one cat that a new breed was developed. It is a disadvantage to the cat not to have hair because it is not protected from the elements. It also doesn't have whiskers, which means it is missing one of its sensory organs. This is an example of breed creation using recessive genes. Emotions run high both for and against this kind of breeding.

NAME:	MAINE COON CAT *(Felis catus)*
WHERE THE BREED DEVELOPED:	UNITED STATES OF AMERICA
COLOR IT:	TYPICALLY A BLACK AND BROWNISH PATTERN THAT WOULD REMIND ONE OF A "RACOON," BUT CAN BE ANY COLOR OR PATTERN. EYES MAY BE GREEN OR COMPLEMENT THE COAT COLOR.
PHYSICAL CHARACTERISTICS:	This interesting cat is large, has long legs, and a long body. The long hair is shorter than a Persian's, but it is longer than the short-hair breeds. The hair is longer around the rump area. The medium-size, tapered head has large ears and large, slanting eyes. The tail tapers, but is blunt ended.
INTERESTING FACTS:	The Maine Coon Cat has a large appearance because it can weigh up to 30 pounds! That is very large for a domestic cat. The breed probably developed as a result of uncontrolled breeding between American domestic cats and Angoras or other long-hair cats. Although it is not popular anywhere else, it is very popular in the eastern United States. There is even a show every year which is exclusively for the shy Maine Coon Cat.

NAME:	JAPANESE BOBTAIL *(Felis catus)*
WHERE THE BREED DEVELOPED:	JAPAN
COLOR IT:	BLACK, RED-BROWN, AND WHITE. EYES ARE A REDDISH-BROWN.
PHYSICAL CHARACTERISTICS:	The Japanese Bobtail is the only cat to have a body that is both sturdily built with well-developed muscles and slender. The hind legs are longer than the front legs but, because the hind legs are kept bent, the back remains level. The large, oval eyes are set on a slant. The large ears and long nose form a perfect equilateral triangle (three sides equal).
INTERESTING FACTS:	The distinctive little tail of the Japanese Bobtail is four or five inches long. Because it is curled up, it looks like it's only two inches long. The hair on the tail sticks out in every direction, giving it the appearance of a rabbit's tail. Even though this breed is relatively unknown in America, it is a very well-known ancient breed. Its likeness is used in Japanese art. The Japanese Bobtail has a soft, silky coat that does not shed as much as most other breeds.

NAME:	TURKISH CAT (ORIGINALLY VAN CAT) *(Felis catus)*
WHERE THE BREED DEVELOPED:	AROUND LAKE VAN IN TURKEY
COLOR IT:	WHITE. REDDISH-BROWN TAIL AND MARKINGS ON HEAD. PINK NOSE AND INSIDE OF EARS. COPPER EYES.
PHYSICAL CHARACTERISTICS:	The Turkish Cat has a long, sturdy body with muscular shoulders and neck. Its large ears are set close together on a wedge-shaped head. The beautiful white coat is long, soft, and silky. The wooly undercoat adds to the fluffy appearance. The full tail is of average length.
INTERESTING FACTS:	This cat was not introduced into Europe until 1955 and is still unknown in the United States, but has been popular for centuries in Turkey. It is relatively unknown because the litters are so small that the breed is very hard to obtain. People that are lucky enough to have these cats know them to be intelligent and affectionate pets. The Turkish Cat's body temperature is 101°F. Cats usually dislike water, but this cat loves to play in water if it is warmed to its body temperature. It has even earned the nickname "swimming cat."

Educational Coloring Books and
STORY CASSETTES

The only non-fiction coloring book/cassette packages available! The cassettes are not read-alongs. Rather, the educational factual information in the coloring book is utilized and enhanced to create exciting stories. Sound, music, and professional narration stimulate interest and promote reading. Children can color and listen, color alone, or simply listen to the cassette. We are proud to offer these quality products at a reasonable price.

DISPLAY RACKS AVAILABLE. INDIVIDUALLY PACKAGED.

YOUR CHOICE OF 48 TITLES

"ISBN (INTERNATIONAL STANDARD BOOK NUMBER) PREFIX ON ALL BOOKS AND CASSETTES: 0-86545-

No.	Title	No.	Title	No.	Title
082-X	DINOSAURS	161-3	DOGS		
083-8	Prehistoric SEA LIFE	162-1	HORSES		
084-6	Prehistoric BIRDS	159-1	BIRDS		
085-4	CAVE MAN	147-8	PENGUINS		
086-2	Prehistoric FISH	098-6	STATE BIRDS		
087-0	Prehistoric MAMMALS	163-X	STATE FLOWERS		
097-8	Count/Color DINOSAURS	100-1	MAMMALS		
089-7	PLAINS INDIANS	101-X	REPTILES		
090-0	NORTHEAST INDIANS	158-3	POISONOUS SNAKES		
091-9	NORTHWEST INDIANS	102-8	CATS OF THE WILD		
092-7	SOUTHEAST INDIANS	103-6	ENDANGERED SPECIES		
093-5	SOUTHWEST INDIANS	157-5	PRIMATES		
094-3	CALIFORNIA INDIANS	104-4	ANIMAL GIANTS		
153-2	ESKIMOS	148-6	ATLANTIC FISH		
152-4	COWBOYS	149-4	PACIFIC FISH		
150-8	COLONIES	105-2	SHARKS	111-7	SPACE EXPLORERS
151-6	PIONEERS	106-0	WHALES	112-5	PLANETS
154-0	FARM ANIMALS	107-9	DEEP-SEA FISH	113-3	COMETS
095-1	DOLLS	108-7	DOLPHINS	114-1	ROCKETS
096-X	ANIMAL ALPHABET	109-5	AIRCRAFT	155-9	TRANSPORTATION
160-5	CATS	110-9	SPACE CRAFT	156-7	SHIPS

ALL BOOK CASSETTE PACKAGES $4.98 EACH

LISTEN AND COLOR
LIBRARY ALBUMS
6 Educational Coloring Books
Book/Story Cassettes
In a plastic storage case

We have gathered cassettes and books of related subject matter into individual library albums. Each album will provide a new, in-depth, and lasting learning experience. They are presented in a beautiful binder that will store and protect your collection for years.

We also invite you to pick 6 titles of your chosing and create your own **CUSTOM ALBUM.**

LIBRARY ALBUMS $34.95 EACH

CHOOSE ANY LIBRARY ALBUM LISTED, OR SELECT TITLES FOR YOUR CUSTOM ALBUM

No. 088-9 Prehistoric Life	No. 116-8 American Indian	No. 164-8 Oceans & Seas	No. 117-6 Air & Space	No. 165-6 Americana
Dinosaurs	Plains Indians	Atlantic Fish	Aircraft	Colonies
Prehistoric Sea Life	Northeast Indians	Pacific Fish	Space Craft	Cowboys
Prehistoric Fish	Northwest Indians	Sharks	Space Explorers	Pioneers
Prehistoric Birds	Southeast Indians	Whales	Planets	State Flowers
Prehistoric Mammals	Southwest Indians	Deep-Sea Fish	Comets	State Birds
Cave Man	California Indians	Dolphins	Rockets	Endangered Species

No. 166-4 Animal Libr #1	No. 167-2 Animal Libr. #2	No. 168-0 Young Students	No. 170-2 New Titles Library	No. 169-9 Custom Libra
Poisonous Snakes	Prehistoric Mammals	Animal Alphabet	Eskimos	WE INVITE YOU TO PIC
Reptiles	Birds	Counting & Coloring Dinosaurs	State Flowers	6 TITLES OF YOU
Animal Giants	Farm Animals	Dolls	Penguins	CHOSING AND CREAT
Mammals	Endangered Species	Dogs	Atlantic Fish	YOUR OWN CUSTO
Cats of the Wild	Animal Alphabet	Cats	Pacific Fish	LIBRARY.
Primates	State Birds	Horses	Farm Animals	